KT-225-951

CONTENTS

CHAPTER 1

A BORN STORYTELLER

(Above)
J. K. Rowling waves to the crowd in Toronto before starting to read from her book.

ON AN AUTUMN DAY IN 2000, a rowdy crowd of twenty thousand people poured into the SkyDome in Toronto, Canada. They were there for a big event. When the lights went down, the noise inside the Dome rose. Finally, the moment everyone was waiting for had arrived. At first, the crowd roared, but then a hush fell over the stadium. A small woman with blond hair shyly stepped onto a stage. She opened a book and started to read. Her

J. K. ROWLING

COLLEEN A. SEXTON

**In Consultation with Martha Cosgrove,
M.A. and Reading Specialist**

LERNER PUBLICATIONS COMPANY/MINNEAPOLIS

Martha Cosgrove has a master's degree from the University of Minnesota in secondary education, with an emphasis on developmental and remedial reading. She is licensed in 7–12 English and language arts, developmental reading, and remedial reading. She has had several works published, and she gives numerous state and national presentations in her areas of expertise.

Copyright © 2006 by Colleen A. Sexton

All rights reserved. International copyright secured. No part of this book may be reproduced, stored in a retrieval system, or transmitted in any form or by any means—electronic, mechanical, photocopying, recording, or otherwise—without the prior written permission of Lerner Publishing Group, except for the inclusion of brief quotations in an acknowledged review.

Lerner Publications Company
A division of Lerner Publishing Group
241 First Avenue North
Minneapolis, Minnesota 55401 U.S.A.

Website address: www.lernerbooks.com

Library of Congress Cataloging-in-Publication Data

Sexton, Colleen A., 1967–
    J.K. Rowling / by Colleen A. Sexton.
       p.   cm. – (Just the facts biographies)
    Includes bibliographical references (p.   ) and index.
    ISBN-13: 978-0-8225-3423-5 (lib. bdg. : alk. paper)
    ISBN-10: 0-8225-3423-1 (lib. bdg. : alk. paper)
    1. Rowling, J. K.–Juvenile literature. 2. Authors, English–20th century–
Biography–Juvenile literature. 3. Potter, Harry (Fictitious character)–
Juvenile literature. 4. Children's stories–Authorship–Juvenile literature.
I. Title. II. Series.
PR6068.O93Z8553   2006
823'.914–dc22   2005017325

Manufactured in the United States of America
1 2 3 4 5 6 – BP – 11 10 09 08 07 06

words brought to life the magical world she had created. This was the largest crowd ever gathered for an author reading. The woman in the center of the frenzy was British writer J. K. Rowling.

Growing up in England, Rowling always knew she wanted to become a writer. She wrote her first story when she was six years old. She filled notebooks with more stories during her school years. Rowling's teachers said she had a great imagination. In 1990, an idea popped into her head. Rowling saw a boy named Harry Potter. He was an orphan who learns at the age of eleven that he is a wizard.

The idea of this boy wizard stuck with Rowling. Over the next few years, she outlined seven novels that would tell Harry's story. During this time, she also married and divorced. She became a single parent and a teacher. And for a short while, she lived in poverty. In 1995, Rowling finished the first manuscript, *Harry Potter and the Philosopher's Stone.* Twelve publishers rejected her work. Then one took a risk and published her book in 1997.

That was only the beginning. Both children and adults followed Harry into his magical world. There, he finds loyal friends and studies how to be a wizard. He also must fight an evil enemy.

By 2005, Rowling had written five more novels. She became the highest-paid author in history. Her fortune is worth about $1 billion. This shy and funny writer had become one of the most influential people in the world.

Rowling connects with kids. She remembers how she felt when she was a child. She writes from those feelings, and she doesn't talk down to kids. Her books are long. But children soak up every word of Harry Potter's fantastic adventures. They dig into their own pockets for the money to buy a book. J. K. Rowling has done what many people never thought possible. She's made reading cool.

EARLY DAYS

In the summer of 1964, two dark-haired strangers stepped onto a train at King's Cross Station in London, England. Pete Rowling was in the Royal Navy. Anne Volant was a member of the Women's Royal Naval Service. Both Pete and Anne were eighteen years old. They were traveling to their new assignments at Arbroath on the east coast of Scotland. Pete chose a seat next to Anne's, and the pair started to talk. When Anne complained of being cold, Pete shared his coat. Nine hours later,

Pete and Anne hopped off the train together. They were in love.

Soon Pete and Anne decided that a life in the navy wasn't for them. So they left the service and married. Pete and Anne wanted to live in the country. They moved to Yate, a small farming and mining village in southwestern England. The Rowlings found a one-story home on Sundridge Park, a winding street near open fields.

Rowling's parents lived in this home in the British village of Yate.

Pete and Anne were eager to have a family. Pete was hardworking and had a lot of energy. He found a job as an apprentice engineer at an aircraft engine company. As an apprentice, Pete learned engineering by working on the production line. Anne gardened, kept a spotless house, and prepared for the birth of their first child.

On July 31, 1965, Anne gave birth to a girl at Cottage Hospital in Yate. The proud parents called their light-haired daughter Joanne Rowling. They didn't give her a middle name. Soon everyone called Joanne by her nickname, Jo. Nearly two years later, the Rowlings had another daughter. They named the dark-haired, dark-eyed baby Diane, or Di for short.

LIFE IN WINTERBOURNE

When Jo was four years old, the Rowlings moved into a modern, three-bedroom house. It was on Nicholls Lane in nearby Winterbourne. Open fields still dotted this growing suburb. The Rowlings settled into life in Winterbourne. Pete made the short trip to nearby Bristol every day. He was among ten thousand workers employed at the airplane engine plant there. Pete worked long days. Soon he moved off the assembly line and became a manager.

Many children lived in the new neighborhood. Their mothers often gathered for a chat over tea while the children played. Two of these playmates were a brother and a sister, Ian and Vikki Potter. Jo especially liked their last name. Names fascinated Jo. She tucked them away in her mind as she grew up.

Jo's mother kept order in a hectic household and seemed to have endless energy. She swam and played guitar. She danced to records by the Beatles. And she took long walks with the family dog, Thumper. Anne became an expert cook who made sure her family ate meals together. When she wasn't rushing around, Anne was reading. Jo remembers that her mother would read anything. Anne's love of books rubbed off on her daughters, especially Jo. She became a storyteller who often directed plays based on her stories. Di always had a starring role.

IT'S A FACT!

Some people thought Rowling's childhood friend Ian Potter inspired the character of Harry. Rowling later wrote to Ian's mother, Ruby Potter. Rowling said she used the family's last name, but the character of Harry came completely from her imagination.

Jo started school when she was five years old. On her first day, she dressed in a red and gray uniform. Then she and her mother made the five-minute walk to Saint Michael's Church of England School. Soon Jo grew to love her little school. So did Di when she was old enough to join her sister.

IT'S A FACT!

On Rowling's first day of school, she still hadn't quite figured out what "going to school" meant. After finishing her first day, she believed she was finished with school forever.

Every afternoon, Anne met her daughters after school for the short walk home. Sometimes they took detours to the duck pond. Or they visited the horses and donkeys at the village stables.

Jo's love of stories grew even stronger during her early school years. She wrote her first book when she was six years old. It was titled "Rabbit" and was about a character of the same name. Rabbit came down with the measles. His friends stopped by to perk up his spirits. One of these friends was a giant bumblebee named Miss Bee. "I gave [the book] to my mother," Jo remembered. "And she said 'That's lovely,' as a mother would, 'That's very, very good.' I stood there and thought, 'Well, get it published then.'"

A MOVE AND A LOSS

Jo turned nine years old in 1974. That same year, her parents discovered an old house in the village of Tutshill. Pete had always wanted to fix up an old house. And Church Cottage in Tutshill was a perfect choice. Built in 1848, Church Cottage was the village school until a larger school was needed.

The Rowlings' home in Tutshill was called Church Cottage. In Britain, old houses often have names instead of street addresses.

Anne and Pete snatched it up and made plans to move from Winterbourne.

Tutshill is near an old forest filled with oaks, beeches, and pine trees. The Rowlings had a beautiful view from their new home. The cottage stood next to Saint Luke's Church and its cemetery. "All our friends thought it was spooky living next to a graveyard," remembered Jo, "but we liked it. I still love graveyards—they are a great

The Rowlings lived next to Saint Luke's Church in Tutshill.

source of names." Jo and Di's new school was the Tutshill Church of England School. The building sat only yards away from their home.

When the fall term started, Jo took a seat in a small, old-fashioned classroom. Her new teacher was Sylvia Morgan. Mrs. Morgan was very stern. She terrified Jo. Mrs. Morgan's first task for the class was a math test. Jo didn't get a single answer right. She hadn't yet learned fractions. Mrs. Morgan sorted her students by how smart she thought they were. Those she believed to be bright sat on her left. Those she thought less smart sat on her right. "It took me a few days to realize I was in the 'stupid' row," Jo recalled. "I was as far right as you could get without sitting in the playground."

Jo's first days in Tutshill became more difficult when her favorite grandparent died. Kathleen Rowling died suddenly of a heart attack. Jo adored her grandmother. It was a treat for Jo and Di to stay with their grandmother and their grandfather, Ernie. The couple ran a grocery store and lived above it. During visits, the girls spent hours playing shop with real cans of food and real money.

INSPIRING PEOPLE

Many of J. K. Rowling's characters are loosely based on people from her childhood. Mrs. Morgan was one of several people who inspired Professor Severus Snape. Aunt Marge is thought to be a bit like Rowling's grandmother Frieda Volant. Rowling says her grandmother was obsessed with dogs. Rowling included her grandfathers, Stan Volant and Ernie Rowling, in *Prisoner of Azkaban.* They became Stan and Ernie, the Knight Bus drivers who rescue Harry from Privet Drive.

Jo and Di's other grandparents were Stanley and Frieda Volant. Jo recalled that Stanley was "a great dreamer, and spent a lot of time in his garden shed, making things." Frieda was a dog lover. She seemed to prefer her four-legged friends to people.

Jo soon settled into her new life and her new school in Tutshill. She and Di explored the fields and the banks of the nearby River Wye. They also joined a club called the Brownies. The girls learned about safety, first aid, and community service. The Brownies often planned special events, such as Christmas and Halloween parties for the elderly. At school, Jo had proved that she was a good student. By the end of the school year, Mrs. Morgan had moved Jo from her seat on the right to one on the left. But this shift had one big downside. "Mrs. Morgan made me swap seats with my best friend, so that in one short walk across the room I became clever but unpopular," Jo later recalled.

CHAPTER 2
A Burning Ambition

PEOPLE OFTEN COMPARED Jo and Di to each other because they were so close in age. Di was known as the pretty and lively sister. Jo had reddish hair and thick glasses that perched on her freckly face. She was the serious and studious sister. Jo was insecure and worried a lot, but she acted confident to cover it up. "I always felt I had to achieve, my hand always had to be the first to go up, I always had to be right," Jo said. "Maybe it was because I felt quite plain in comparison to my sister. I probably felt I had to compensate."

Books filled the nooks and crannies of Church Cottage. Jo read anything she could get her hands on. Her favorite book was *The Little White Horse*, by Elizabeth Goudge. This story is about a plain-looking orphan girl who goes to live with her uncle in his English manor. Jo also loved *Black Beauty, Little Women,* and *I Capture the Castle*. She enjoyed books in the *Chronicles of Narnia* series by C. S. Lewis. By the age of nine, she was reading some adult books. They included Ian Fleming's novels about the British spy James Bond.

These books and others inspired Jo to work on her writing. She spent more time developing characters and creating detailed plots. One of her early efforts was an adventure story titled "The Seven Cursed Diamonds." "I always, always wanted to be a writer but I *never* shared my burning ambition with anyone,"

IT'S A FACT!

As a child, Rowling rarely shared her writing with anyone but Di. But she never minded showing off her drawings and paintings. Rowling still draws for pleasure. And she often makes small sketches when she's thinking about how a character or magical object looks.

remembered Jo. She didn't share her dream, but Jo did show her stories to her sister. Di always told her to keep writing.

WYEDEAN COMPREHENSIVE SCHOOL

Jo started to lose some of her seriousness in her early teenage years. By this time, she and her sister both wore the yellow and brown uniform of Wyedean Comprehensive. This public high school was in the nearby village of Sedbury. Jo quickly fell into a group of smart and studious friends. The girls spent their lunch periods listening to Jo tell soap opera-type stories. "They usually involved us all doing heroic and daring deeds we certainly wouldn't have done in real life; we were all too swotty [nerdy]," Jo recalled.

Jo wasn't good at subjects she thought were practical, like metalworking, woodworking, and gym. But she received high marks for her writing from her English teachers. Jo's favorite English teacher, Lucy Shepherd, was an inspiration. Miss Shepherd cared about her students' progress and had high expectations. "I really respected her because she was a teacher who was passionate about teaching us. She was an introduction to a different kind of woman, I suppose. She was a feminist, and clever," Jo recalled. From Miss Shepherd, Jo learned that structure and pacing were important in writing. She began to make her writing more precise.

Books continued to influence Jo. She loved the novels of Jane Austen, who wrote in the 1800s. Austen's main characters were often sisters who had to deal with the limits of Britain's upper-class society. Jo read Austen's *Emma* again and again. And she picked up William Thackeray's *Vanity Fair*. But it was Jessica Mitford's autobiographical work, *Hons and Rebels*, that inspired Jo most.

Rowling looked up to Jessica Mitford (left), a writer and activist.

JESSICA MITFORD

Jessica Mitford was born into a wealthy British family in 1917. Her brother attended top schools. Her mother educated Jessica and her sisters at home. Mitford ran away from home when she was nineteen years old to marry Esmond Romilly. He was a man she greatly admired for fighting the Fascists during the Spanish Civil War (1936–1939). Fascism was a political movement. Fascists favor a government led by a dictator who has unlimited power.

Mitford and her husband moved to the United States. Romilly became a U.S. soldier. He fought in World War II (1939–1945) and was killed in 1941. Mitford went to work in a government office. She also joined the Communist Party. Communists support a type of government that controls the economy and works to share all goods equally among the people.

In 1943, Mitford married lawyer Robert Treuhaft. He was also a member of the Communist Party. The couple settled in Oakland, California. Together, Mitford and her husband worked for the Civil Rights Congress. Its goal was to gain civil rights—such as better working and living conditions—for all people.

Mitford then turned to writing. Jo Rowling especially liked Mitford's autobiography *Hons and Rebels*. Mitford was known for her charm and wit. She soon gained fame as a journalist. People knew she was someone who would always look for the truth. Her work inspired other people to actively support civil rights. She continued to write until her death in 1996.

Mitford was a social activist who ran away from her wealthy family. She bought a camera and went traveling. She wrote about people who didn't have the right to say what they felt. Writing was Mitford's way of actively working for social justice.

Jo was fascinated by this rebel and admired Mitford's spirit of adventure. "She had tremendous moral courage and did some physically brave things as a human rights activist. I love her sense of humor, her great independence," Jo later said.

DIFFICULT NEWS

Anne Rowling took a job at her daughters' school as a laboratory assistant in the chemistry department. She especially liked being around the students. The job also gave her time to spend with her daughters. The threesome made the trip to and from school each day.

Around this time, Anne started having trouble lifting things. She sometimes felt the pricks of "pins and needles" in her right arm. Other times, her arm felt numb and weak. At first, Anne dismissed the feeling as minor aches and pains. Within a few years, the pain had spread.

Anne was thirty-five years old when her doctor told her she had multiple sclerosis (MS). This incurable disease attacks the nervous system. The attacks are unpredictable. People who have MS can experience loss of balance, numbness, and weakness. Some patients are very tired all the time. Some lose their eyesight. Most people with MS go through long periods when they feel well. This is called remission. But some patients can become seriously disabled in a short amount of time.

Anne did not seem to have periods of recovery. Her illness grew slowly but steadily worse. At the age of fifteen, Jo had trouble accepting the news of her mother's illness. "I think most people believe, deep down, that their mothers are indestructible; it was a terrible shock to hear that she had an incurable illness, but even then, I did not fully realize what the diagnosis might mean," Jo recalled. Anne cheerfully worked to keep life at Church Cottage unchanged. The house was as clean as ever. And she kept up her job at Wyedean Comprehensive for as long as she could.

Still, life at Church Cottage was often sad. It was hard for Jo to be at home sometimes. She turned to her friends for comfort and fun. She also worked harder at her studies. During Jo's last years at Wyedean, she focused on her English classes. She also studied the French and German languages. Jo became more interested in music too. She played the guitar and had daydreams of playing an electric guitar solo. Jo had always liked the Beatles and became a big fan of the punk band the Clash. In the punk style, she wore heavy black eye makeup. Jo and her friends sometimes went to dances for teens. But Tutshill didn't offer much excitement. Jo was often bored and restless.

FINDING FREEDOM

Jo found a cure for her boredom in Sean Harris. This boy started at Wyedean during Jo's last year there. Sean and Jo became instant and lifelong friends. Unlike Jo, Sean knew how to drive. He had a turquoise and white Ford Anglia. Sean and Jo hit the

IT'S A FACT!
Rowling admits that Sean Harris was the inspiration for Ron Weasley. She dedicated the second Harry Potter book to him.

highways in the car. They headed for fun in the clubs and discos of Bristol, Newport, and other bigger towns. "Some of the happiest memories of my teenage years involve zooming off into the darkness in Sean's car," Jo remembered.

Jo felt she could share her hopes and dreams with Sean. He was the first person Jo told about her ambition to be a writer. Sean believed in Jo's abilities and said he was sure she'd be a big success. Sean's support meant a lot to Jo.

Jo continued to earn outstanding grades and was popular in school. She graduated with honors from Wyedean in 1983. Her greatest goal was to be a writer. And she had a strong desire to fight for changes in society like her idol, Jessica Mitford. She left behind her quiet life at Church Cottage and set out for the University of Exeter.

A NEW WORLD

The University of Exeter is on the southern coast of England. The school was only a two-hour drive from Jo's home in Tutshill. But the campus was a whole new world to Jo. The dorm where she lived was small and cramped. And Jo was

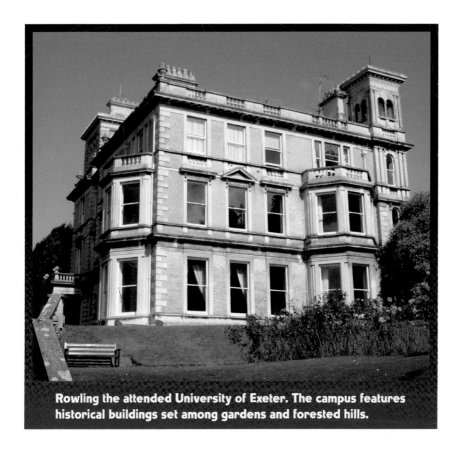

Rowling the attended University of Exeter. The campus features historical buildings set among gardens and forested hills.

just one of many students who had been smart and popular in their hometown schools.

Jo met many of her friends at Devonshire House, Exeter's student union. She became a regular at the coffee bar there. It was a good place to meet friends and talk. Jo loved the freedom of college life, and she became more outgoing. She dated and soon had a serious boyfriend. Still, she enjoyed spending time with just her female friends. As she had at Wyedean, Jo told stories that featured her friends as the main characters. And music was as important as ever. About this time, Jo discovered the Smiths. This band quickly became her all-time favorite group. She tried to play the band's sad tunes on her guitar.

IT'S A FACT!

Rowling's teachers at Exeter thought she was only an average student. In fact, her grade point average was only 2.2 while she was there. This is the same as a C+.

At Exeter, Jo wasn't a star student as she had been at Wyedean. She didn't study as hard and was a bit of a daydreamer.

All the same, she loved her university classes about the mythology, history, and literature of ancient Greece and Rome. Her main course of study was French. She spent a year in France to learn about the culture and more about the language. In her last year at Exeter, she worked hard on a long paper called a dissertation. Jo wrote this three-thousand-word paper in French as part of earning her degree.

Rowling read books by J. R. R. Tolkien (left) during her college years.

Throughout her college years, Jo continued to write stories and even a little poetry. She also fed her mind with more books. *A Tale of Two Cities* by Charles Dickens and *The Lord of the Rings* trilogy by J. R. R. Tolkien were among the many works she read.

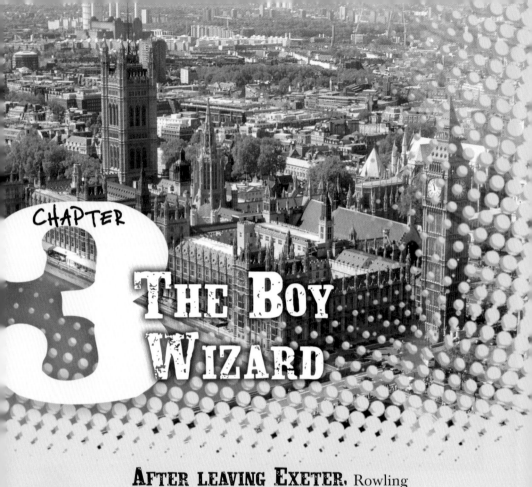

3 THE BOY WIZARD

AFTER LEAVING EXETER, Rowling moved to London to find a career. She took a secretarial class for people skilled in foreign languages. Then Rowling accepted a job doing research for Amnesty International. This organization works to protect human rights and social justice around the world. These rights include everyone being equal before the law and freedom of speech. Rowling helped research cases of human rights abuse in French-speaking African countries.

Rowling moved to London *(above)* in 1987.

She found her work interesting, but she didn't think she was very good at it. She was too disorganized. Also, writing drew her attention away from her work. Rowling had started a novel for adults and spent every spare minute working on it. Whenever her coworkers asked her to lunch, she made excuses and raced off to a café. There, she would jot down some notes or plot out a chapter. Cafés became her favorite places to write.

After two years of doing research at Amnesty International, Rowling became tired of working in an office behind the scenes. She wanted to work on the front lines in the fight for social justice. But there were no opportunities for her. Rowling quit and went to work as a secretary. She drifted from one job to another. For a short time, Rowling was a secretary at a publishing company. She typed letters to authors whose manuscripts were rejected. Rowling also gave up on one novel she was writing and went on to another. She didn't think either book was good enough to publish.

Rowling became a fast typist. But in all other areas, she proved to be "the worst secretary ever." To her, being a secretary was just a way to support herself while she worked on her writing.

ADVICE TO YOUNG WRITERS

J. K. Rowling always knew she wanted to be a writer. She feels lucky that she can make a living doing what she does best. But her success took planning and hard work. It took some luck too. Young writers often ask her for advice. She tells them, "Read as much as you can. Keep writing and throwing it away until one day you do something that you don't think belongs in the [trash] bin. Stick to writing what you know about. Don't give up."

"All I ever liked about working in offices was being able to type up stories on the computer when no one was looking," Rowling said. "I was never paying much attention in meetings because I was usually scribbling bits of my latest stories in the margins of the pad, or choosing excellent names for the characters."

AN IDEA

In 1990, Rowling decided to move to Manchester, where her boyfriend lived. This large, industrial city is in northern England. On weekends, Rowling began to search for an apartment there. One day in June, she was returning home to London by train. She sat by a window and watched the countryside go by. All of sudden, the image of a dark-haired boy popped into her mind. He was scrawny, and he had green eyes and round glasses. A lightning bolt-shaped mark streaked across his forehead. The boy was a wizard, but he didn't know it yet. He would learn to be a wizard at a wizarding school. "It was the purest stroke of inspiration I've ever had in my life," Rowling later said.

Rowling didn't have a pen or a piece of paper with her. And she was too shy to borrow them from another passenger. Since she couldn't write down her thoughts, she closed her eyes and let her imagination go. "I think that perhaps if I had had to slow down the ideas so that I could capture them on paper I might have stifled some of them," Rowling later noted. The train broke down for four hours midway to London. Rowling had all this time to get to know the boy she would later name Harry Potter.

First, Rowling thought about where Harry would go to school. It would be a big and mysterious castle. Rowling would later name it Hogwarts School of Witchcraft and Wizardry. She thought the school should be in an out-of-the-way place. The rugged landscape of northern Scotland seemed perfect. Rowling was familiar with many

By the time Rowling's train arrived at King's Cross Station (*above*), she had started planning her story about a boy wizard.

ancient castles. But, she said, "I have never seen a castle anywhere that looks the way I imagine Hogwarts."

Rowling finally stepped off the train at King's Cross Station in London. By this time, she knew she would write seven books. She would write one book for each year the boy wizard went to school at Hogwarts. Rowling had also dreamed up Harry's friend Ron Weasley and the school gamekeeper Hagrid. She knew that the school would have ghosts too. Peeves and Nearly Headless Nick were part of her plans right from the start.

IT'S A FACT!
Rowling describes Hagrid as a Hell's Angels motorcyclist who gardens in his backyard.

Rowling started to work on her new idea that very night. "I spent a lot of time inventing the rules for the magical world so that I knew the limits of magic," Rowling later noted. "Then I had to invent the different ways wizards could accomplish certain things. Some of the magic in the books is based on what people used to believe really worked, but most of it is my invention." Rowling saw her work as research. She had to find out who Harry Potter was. His parents had lived in the wizarding world. How did they die? And why didn't Harry know he was a wizard? How had he come to live with his non-magical aunt and uncle? And what would happen to him during his years at Hogwarts? Rowling would spend five years figuring out the answers to these questions and many more. She developed the characters and plots for all seven books before she even finished writing the first book.

CHARACTERS FIRST

The characters came first. Rowling wrote a life history for nearly all of them. She knew she could not put all this information in her books. But she felt that she needed to know her characters inside out before writing about them. All her life, Rowling had collected unusual names. So she had plenty of names to pluck out of her mind for her characters. And she kept looking for more. Nothing pleased her as much as looking over a long list of names. "For me it's like casting an eye over a pile of unwrapped presents, each of the names representing a whole person. War

Rowling created the characters and setting for Harry Potter's adventures. Then she started writing the story.

memorials, telephone directories, shop fronts, saints, villains, baby-naming books–you name it, I've got names from it!" Rowling later said.

It didn't take long to find a name for her main character. "Harry" had always been one of Rowling's favorite boy's names. His last name, however, took a little longer. Rowling tried out several before choosing "Potter," the last name of her childhood friends in Winterbourne. Harry Potter is famous in the magical world as "the boy who lived." The dark wizard Voldemort killed Harry's parents, James and Lily Potter. Harry was just a baby, but he survived the attack. Voldemort disappeared after the attack. He was weakened after trying to kill Harry. The only evidence left of the attack is the lightning bolt-shaped scar that Voldemort's wand left on Harry's forehead.

Rowling put some of herself into Harry. They were both born on July 31. Harry tends to be quiet and serious, just as Rowling was as a child. She imagined Harry as a bit of an old soul. He is wise and understanding beyond his years. Harry is also sensible, a loyal friend, and very brave. Rowling admires bravery more than any other trait. Unlike Rowling, Harry is good at sports. He's a standout at the popular wizarding game Quidditch. At Hogwarts, Harry is just an average student who does not work as hard as he could. He is naturally good at some subjects, such as Defense Against the Dark Arts. But he's awful at others, especially Potions. Harry has faults too. He can be proud and stubborn. Sometimes he thinks only of himself and acts before thinking.

Harry's best friend is red-haired Ron Weasley. As Rowling wrote about Ron, she realized that he was much like her friend Sean Harris. "Although I never meant him to be like Sean, once I got Ron onto the page he often behaved like my oldest friend, who is both very funny and deeply loyal," she said. In many ways, Ron has a life Harry has always wanted. Ron is a typical boy. He grew up with two loving parents. He has a younger sister and five older brothers. Being the youngest of six brothers is hard for Ron. He often feels unimportant. He struggles to find one talent that will set him apart from his siblings. The Weasleys' lack of money often embarrasses Ron. His clothes and belongings are usually worn hand-me-downs. But he has a home full of laughter and happiness, something Harry longs for.

The character of Hermione (pronounced Her-my-o-nee) Granger rounds out the three friends who are at the center of Rowling's story. The name Hermione came from the name of a character in Shakespeare's play *The Winter's Tale.* At first, Hermione Granger had the last name Puckle. But Rowling decided that such a smart girl needed a name that better suited her serious nature. Hermione is plain looking and has brown hair and brown eyes. An only child, she comes from a loving, non-magical family. Hermione has a great fear of failure. So she studies hard to be the best and brightest student at Hogwarts. Hermione is often an annoying know-it-all. She lectures her friends when they do something wrong. But she is also kindhearted, clever, and loyal. Of all the characters, Hermione is

The characters Hermione *(left)*, Harry *(center)*, and Ron *(right)* later came to life in movies based on Rowling's books.

the most like Rowling herself. "Hermione is me, near enough," Rowling later said. "I wasn't that clever. But I was that annoying on occasion."

Who Is Who, What Is What

Draco Malfoy: Harry's worst enemy at Hogwarts

Gryffindor: a house at Hogwarts founded by Godric Gryffindor. Harry, Ron, and Hermione belong to this house.

Hagrid: a great friend to Harry, Ron, and Hermione. He looks after the grounds of Hogwarts and takes care of magical creatures.

Harry Potter: a Gryffindor student whose parents were killed fighting Voldemort. Harry is the central character in all the books.

Hermione Granger: Harry's best female friend

Hogwarts: the school where students learn to be wizards or witches

Hufflepuff: a house at Hogwarts founded by Helga Hufflepuff

Muggle: a person from the non-magical world

Professor Dumbledore: the head master (principal) of Hogwarts

Professor McGonagall: the head of Gryffindor House

Professor Snape: the head of Slytherin House

Ravenclaw: a house at Hogwarts founded by Rowena Ravenclaw

Ron Weasley: Harry's best male friend

Slytherin: a house at Hogwarts founded by Salazar Slytherin

Voldemort: a former Slytherin student who uses his wizarding skills to do evil

Harry would be the hero of Rowling's story. But he would need Ron's and Hermione's support to get through Hogwarts. The friendship among these three characters would be important to the story. They would be brave. They would have faith in one another. And they would have a strong belief in the power of good over evil. Rowling knew these themes would all be part of her story.

HARRY'S TWO WORLDS

Soon Rowling had boxes crammed with notes on her new project. Her notes traveled with her as she moved to Manchester. Rowling took a secretarial job there.

Rowling was very busy working and spending time with her boyfriend. She also had to learn her way around a new city. But she spent every spare moment creating Harry Potter's world. Her hero would actually be part of two worlds. He would live in the magical world. And he would live in the world of Muggles. This was the name Rowling gave to non-magical people. Harry's Muggle aunt and uncle would raise him. In the Muggle world, everything is clean and orderly. The houses are well kept. Muggles always follow their daily routines. Anyone who looks or behaves out of the ordinary raises eyebrows. And there is hardly ever any excitement.

In the wizarding world, a surprise lies around every corner. Nothing seems orderly. Houses, buildings, and roads go every which way. People and objects appear and disappear. The people in paintings and photographs wander in and out of view. Mirrors sometimes talk. Ghosts, giants, and elves live in the magical world. Witches and wizards cast spells and fly broomsticks. Goblins run banks. Owls deliver the daily mail. Unicorns, dragons, and centaurs live in the wild. Danger and excitement are everywhere.

Witches and wizards move back and forth between their world and the Muggle world. They dress in capes and other clothing that Muggles disapprove of. "The wizards represent all that the true 'Muggle' most fears: They are plainly outcasts and comfortable with being so." Rowling later said. In the magical world, strict rules control the use of magic around Muggles. Rowling invented a government called the Ministry of Magic. It makes sure witches and wizards follow these rules. But keeping the magical world hidden from the Muggles is difficult. Witches and wizards need to be on guard.

CREATING HOGWARTS

Rowling's ideas about Hogwarts started taking shape. Students travel to the school on a train called the Hogwarts Express. When they arrive, they find a huge stone castle. The school is perched on a high cliff. It overlooks a large lake and an enchanted forest. Mountains surround the castle, which is often shrouded in fog.

Hogwarts looks as mysterious on the inside as it does on the outside. Torches cast light and shadows on the walls inside the castle. Ghosts haunt all corners of the school. Rooms appear and disappear. Staircases change direction without warning. Doors sometimes won't open without being asked politely. The Great Hall is where the students gather

IT'S A FACT!

The real King's Cross Station doesn't have brick walls, even though that's how Rowling described them. She admits she confused the look of King's Cross Station with Euston, another London railway station. Even so, King's Cross has posted a marker between Platforms 9 and 10. It shows where fictional Hogwarts students would rush to Platform 9¾ to get on the Hogwarts Express.

for meals and celebrations. The room's high ceiling is bewitched to look like the sky outside. Dark dungeons and chambers make up the lower levels of the school. Towers rise high into the air.

Four famous wizards established Hogwarts long ago. Students belong to one of four houses named for these founders. Harry, Ron, and Hermione are in Gryffindor. This house is known for its daring and brave wizards. Hufflepuffs are hardworking and loyal. Ravenclaws are wise and witty. Clever and wicked students belong to Slytherin House.

Hogwarts is a place of order and rules. Its motto is "Never Tickle a Sleeping Dragon." These words tell students that breaking the rules could lead to trouble or danger. Students must answer to the headmaster (principal), professors, and staff. The headmaster of Hogwarts is the kind and wise Albus Dumbledore. Professor Dumbledore is a very powerful wizard. Dumbledore is Harry's main protector. The head of Gryffindor House is Professor Minerva McGonagall. She is strict, clever, and fair. She is someone Harry, Ron, and Hermione trust and respect.

The one professor the friends do not trust is Severus Snape. He is the head of Slytherin

Professor Albus Dumbledore is headmaster of Hogwarts and Harry's main protector.

House. Rowling took his last name from a village called Snape, which she found on a map of Britain. Snape strongly dislikes Harry. Dumbledore trusts Snape, but Harry and his friends are suspicious of him.

Rubeus Hagrid is the gamekeeper at Hogwarts. He watches over the magical creatures in Hogwarts' Forbidden Forest. Hagrid becomes a treasured friend to Harry, Ron, and Hermione. Rowling has admitted that Hagrid is one of her favorite characters.

CHAPTER

4 A CHANGE OF SCENERY

SHORTLY BEFORE CHRISTMAS 1990,
Rowling visited her parents in Tutshill. She
noticed that her mother was very tired and
thin. The MS had advanced so far that Anne
needed a wheelchair to get around outside the
house. Indoors, she was unable to go upstairs.
She used a walker to get around the ground
floor of Church Cottage.

On Christmas Eve, Rowling said good-bye to her parents and returned to Manchester. She planned to spend the rest of the holidays with her boyfriend and his family. Then on December 30, the phone rang early in the morning. Rowling knew it was bad news when she heard her father's voice. Her mother had died. Rowling had seen how weak her mother was. But her death was unexpected. "I don't know how I didn't realize how ill she was, except that I had watched her deteriorate for so long that the change, at the time, didn't seem so dramatic," Rowling remembered. Anne was only forty-five.

Rowling's world had suddenly changed. The months that followed were a terrible time in her life. "I remember feeling as though there was a slab [of cement] pressing down upon my chest, a literal pain in my heart," said Rowling. She was only twenty-five years old and felt crushed with grief. To make things worse, her job suddenly ended. She didn't like her new job at the University of Manchester. Her relationship with her boyfriend was falling apart. And then came the last straw. Thieves broke into Rowling's home. They stole everything her mother had left her. Rowling decided it was time to get away.

PORTO

Rowling found a small ad for a job in the newspaper. A school in Porto, Portugal, was looking for English teachers. Rowling applied for the job and got it. Soon she was off to Portugal, where the climate is warm. She was eager for a new challenge and a change of scenery.

Rowling moved into a four-bedroom apartment for the school's teachers. She became instant friends with her new roommates. Aine

Rowling moved to Porto, Portugal, in 1991 to teach English.

Kiely was from Ireland, and Jill Prewett was from England. The three women taught in the evenings. After classes, they had fun at the local bars or discos. Sometimes they talked over dinners of pizza and wine.

Rowling enjoyed teaching English. Her students ranged in age from eight to sixty-two. Some were businesspeople who wanted to further their careers. Others took lessons for fun. Rowling's favorites were teenagers who needed help passing English exams. They were bubbling with ideas and opinions.

Because she worked evenings, Rowling was free to write during the day. She sat in the cafés of Porto with pen and paper. She sipped strong coffee as she wrote her novel in longhand. By this time, Rowling had started drafting her story about Harry Potter. Since her mother's death, however, her young hero had changed. "Harry's feelings about

IT'S A FACT!

Rowling dedicated *Harry Potter and the Prisoner of Azkaban* to her roommates in Portugal, Aine and Jill. The dedication calls them the godmothers of "Swing." This was the name of a local disco where they spent their free time.

Rowling loved to write in cafés.

his dead parents had become much deeper, much more real," Rowling said.

Rowling wrote her favorite chapter of the book during her first weeks in Porto. In "The Mirror of Erised," Harry looks into an enchanted mirror. He sees himself surrounded by his parents and other relatives. They are all smiling and looking proud of Harry. The word *erised* spelled backward is *desire*. In that mirror, Harry saw what his heart most longed for. It was his family. "I only fully realized upon re-reading the book how many of my own feelings about losing my mother I had given Harry," Rowling later said.

FINDING LOVE

One Saturday night, Rowling and her roommates went to a bar called the Meia Cava. They could listen to jazz music at this bar. A Portuguese journalism student named Jorge Arantes was also there with his friends. Rowling's blue eyes drew his attention when she walked into the bar. Arantes spoke English well and struck up a conversation with Rowling. They found that they both loved books. Arantes had read *Sense and Sensibility* by Jane Austen, one of Rowling's favorite writers. She was impressed.

Arantes called Rowling a few days later, and they began dating. Soon they were always together. Rowling moved in with Arantes and his mother, Marília Rodrigues. Mrs. Rodrigues came to think of her son's new girlfriend as part of the family. Rowling seemed happy in her new relationship. She was happier than she had been since her mother's death. Rowling told Arantes about her novel and shared the beginnings of the book with him. He remembers telling her that he was in love with a great writer.

In August of 1992, Arantes asked Rowling to marry him, and she accepted. But the couple's romance showed signs of trouble. They often argued. Still, the couple's plans to marry did not change. Rowling's sister Di flew to Porto from Edinburgh, Scotland, for the wedding. Rowling and Arantes had a small wedding in Porto on the morning of October 16. They didn't go on a honeymoon. In fact, Rowling went to work as usual that evening. She became pregnant within a few weeks. Rowling taught throughout her pregnancy and kept working on Harry Potter. On July 27, 1993, Rowling gave birth to a healthy baby girl. She named her Jessica, after Jessica Mitford. Rowling's new daughter became the best thing in her life. "I was over the moon to be a mother," she remembered.

IT'S A FACT!

Rowling wore black during the marriage ceremony to her first husband, Jorge Arantes.

BREAKING UP

The new baby did not improve Rowling and
Arantes's relationship. In fact, they had more stress
than ever in their lives. Arantes had just finished
eight months of required service in the Portuguese
army. He was looking for a job. Rowling was
supporting the family by herself. And taking care of
a newborn baby was a big responsibility. Rowling
and Arantes were both unhappy with their lives.
The couple often had big arguments. Sometimes the
fighting was physically violent.

In November 1993, the relationship reached a
breaking point. Rowling told Arantes that she did
not love him anymore. He exploded with anger
and forced Rowling out of the house. She was left
standing alone in the street with nothing. She knew
that she had to get her four-month-old daughter
and leave. But she feared that Arantes would keep
Jessica from her. Rowling went to her old
roommates for help. They called a friend named
Maria Inés Aguiar. Aguiar persuaded the police to
accompany her to Arantes's house. The officers
convinced him to give up the baby.

Two weeks later, Rowling and her daughter
were on a flight to London. She wanted to put

distance between herself and her husband. But she did not have a home or a job, and she had very little money. All her possessions fit in two suitcases. Rowling thought about living in London again. Many of her friends lived there. But they were all single and enjoying a carefree life. London didn't feel like the right place for Rowling. Her father had moved away from her childhood home in Tutshill. He had settled with his new wife, Janet Gallivan, in nearby Chepstow. So Rowling decided to go north to Edinburgh. Her sister Di lived there with her husband, Roger Moore, a restaurant owner.

Many feelings were brewing inside Rowling. Most of all, she felt angry with herself. She had left Britain in search of a better and happier life. She was returning with her life in even more turmoil. "I never expected to find myself in that situation, and I was furious with myself," she later recalled. "But I certainly never regretted leaving, and I never ever for a second regretted Jessica. She kept me going."

CHAPTER 5
THE POVERTY TRAP

ROWLING HAD A GOOD FEELING about Edinburgh. The city is Scotland's cultural center and the country's second-largest city. Rowling thought she could be happy there. And it seemed like a good place to bring up her daughter. Rowling knew it would be hard to build a new life and raise Jessica on her

After she left Portugal, Rowling lived in Edinburgh, Scotland (above).

53

own. But she was sure she would be doing fine within a few months. After all, she was well-educated and willing to work hard.

ENDLESS PROBLEMS

Rowling didn't want to be a burden to her sister. So she decided to go on welfare (government assistance). The money from the government would help her pay her bills while she looked for a job. On December 21, 1994, Rowling filled out endless paperwork at the Department of Social Security. The experience was depressing. "You have to be interviewed and explain to a lot of strangers how you came to be penniless and the sole carer of your child," Rowling later described. "I know that nobody was setting out to make me feel humiliated and worthless, though that is exactly how I felt." Her application was accepted. This meant that she would receive money to pay for food, housing, clothing, and other needs.

Rowling rented an apartment and bought some basics with her remaining savings. She soon discovered that mice lived in her walls. The apartment was miserable. But she was determined to make the best of it. Each week, Rowling signed for her public assistance check at the post office.

WELFARE

Britain set up public assistance in the 1950s. The welfare program supports families that do not make enough money to support themselves. Once the person on welfare makes a higher income, the support is taken away. Critics believe the system encourages people to remain unemployed. Supporters believe low-income families need help to give a better life to their children.

Rowling was in the government assistance program for only a short time. She got about one hundred dollars a week. She never forgot the experience. After she had earned a lot of money, she wanted to support one-parent families. In September 2000, Rowling became an ambassador for the National Council for One Parent Families. In 2004, she became president of the organization, which helps single mothers with children. Rowling has also made significant donations over the years.

Rowling pretended to shop in children's clothing stores so that she could pick up the diapers offered for free in changing rooms. And some days, Jessica ate, but Rowling did not.

One day, Rowling knew she had hit rock bottom. She was visiting a friend of her sister's. The friend had a son just a few months older than Jessica. This boy had a beautiful bedroom full of toys. "At that point, when I packed Jessica's toys away, they fitted into a shoebox, literally. I came home and cried my eyes out," Rowling remembered. She could no longer bear the noisy scratching of the mice in the walls. "I just never expected to mess up so badly that I would find myself in an unheated, mouse-infested flat, looking after my daughter. And I was angry because I felt I was letting her down," Rowling later said. So she turned to Sean Harris. He had been a loyal friend through the years. Sean lent Rowling money so that she and Jessica could move. They found a one-bedroom apartment in a better neighborhood.

Rowling wanted to work part-time. But she soon realized that she was stuck in a poverty trap. She couldn't work unless she found child care for Jessica. But Rowling couldn't afford child care unless she had a well-paying job. Rowling didn't qualify for government programs that helped with child care.

WRITING AGAIN

Rowling's daily struggles depressed her. Living in poverty made her feel unsure of herself and her abilities. Rowling turned to her sister Di for comfort. Di's upbeat outlook lifted her older sister's spirits. Rowling mentioned her latest writing project to Di during one visit. Di wanted to hear all about it. Rowling handed her the three chapters of the book that she had completed. Di eagerly started reading it. Soon Di smiled and then laughed out loud. Rowling was relieved. It was exactly the reaction she had been hoping for.

Di's encouraging words helped Rowling make two decisions. First, she would write the novel about Harry Potter. And then she would go to work full-time. Rowling wanted to teach again. But she found that she didn't qualify to teach in Scotland's schools. She needed to earn a special certificate of education. The program lasted a year. Classes would keep her very busy. Rowling knew that if she didn't write the book about Harry Potter now, she might never get it done. "And so I set to work in a kind of frenzy, determined to finish the book and at least try to get it published," Rowling said.

Every day, Rowling and her daughter set out for a nearby park. The fresh air and activity lulled Jessica to sleep. Then Rowling pushed the baby carriage to a café and went to work. Her favorite place to write was Nicolson's. Her brother-in-law was one of the café's owners. Rowling felt comfortable at Nicolson's. She could sit there

IT'S A FACT!

After Nicolson's gained fame as Rowling's favorite writing spot, it was remodeled and sold as a stylish restaurant and bar.

undisturbed for hours with an espresso drink while Jessica napped. Rowling wrote again in the evenings after the baby had gone to sleep.

The only time Rowling stopped writing was when her husband arrived. Jorge Arantes had traveled to Edinburgh from Porto in search of his wife and daughter. Arantes had turned to drugs after Rowling left him. Rowling worried that he would say things to hurt her. She also thought he might physically hurt her. Rowling was concerned about her own well-being as well as Jessica's. In March 1994, she filed papers in court asking for an order that would stop Arantes from seeing his wife and daughter in Edinburgh. The court granted Rowling's request. Arantes returned to Portugal.

Five months later, Rowling filed for a divorce. It would become final in June 1995. At that time, the order against Arantes would also become permanent. "Although things were hard," she later said, "I don't regret the marriage because it gave me my daughter and I would not want to change anything about her."

MAKING PLANS

Things were starting to look up for Rowling by the end of 1994. She was making great progress on Harry Potter. She also found some typing work, which brought in a little money every week.

The end of the Harry Potter novel was in sight. So Rowling started making plans to earn her certificate of education. In January 1995, she applied at a school of education called Moray House. Rowling went through a daylong

Rowling earned her teaching degree at Moray House (left) in Edinburgh.

interview in which she could only speak French. This was the language Rowling wanted to teach. Rowling won a spot in the program. She was thrilled to be accepted to Moray House. It was a big accomplishment that made her feel good about herself.

Rowling tackled her novel with even greater enthusiasm. She had completed a draft of the entire book by the end of the summer. About this time, Rowling also received a grant from the Scottish Office of Education. The grant would help her pay for her schooling and textbooks.

IT'S A FACT!

While Rowling was writing the first Harry Potter book, she also wrote the last chapter of the seventh book. She did this to drive her toward the goal of writing the entire series.

Rowling thought she was as ready as she could be to begin her studies. Then she learned that her new school no longer offered child care. A friend who has never been named came to her rescue and offered a large loan. "I broke down and cried when my friend offered it to me," Rowling later said. "It was this enormous sum of money. I think we both thought I would never be able to pay it back. The friend was saying in effect: 'Here is a gift to help you.'" The grant and the gift from her friend helped Rowling go off welfare.

6 PUBLISHING HARRY POTTER

(Above) Rowling posed for this photo in 1997. Her first book had just been published.

ROWLING POLISHED the first draft of her book over the next several months. In late 1995, the story of Harry Potter's first year at Hogwarts was finished. Rowling typed the whole manuscript on a secondhand manual typewriter. She couldn't afford to photocopy the manuscript, so she typed another copy herself.

Rowling's next challenge was to figure out who might be interested in publishing her story. At the library, she found a reference book that listed publishers and agents. Agents help authors sell their work to publishers. Rowling's eyes slid over the list of names, and one agent stood out. His name was Christopher Little. Rowling liked this name. It sounded like a character in a children's book. So she wrote it down along with a few others.

By this time, Rowling had spent nearly six years creating Harry Potter's world. She knew all the characters that lived there. She had plotted out each of her hero's seven years at Hogwarts. And she knew how Harry Potter's story would end. Now it was time to send Harry out into the world. Rowling was excited and nervous as she put the first three chapters of her book into envelopes. Soon *Harry Potter and the Philosopher's*

IT'S A FACT!

Many agents and publishers in Britain and the United States accept unsolicited manuscripts. These are unpublished works that the agent or publisher has not asked—or solicited— the authors to send in. Unknown authors send in these manuscripts directly for consideration.

Stone, by Joanne Rowling, would be in the hands of publishers and agents.

AN AGENT

A young office manager named Bryony Evens worked at the Christopher Little Literary Agency in London. She was in charge of opening the mail. Every day, she sorted the manuscripts the agency received into piles. Rejected manuscripts went in one pile. Manuscripts for Christopher Little to consider went in another pile. Evens put Rowling's three sample chapters in the reject pile because the agency did not handle children's books. "But it had an interesting binder [folder], with a peculiar fastening," Evens later recalled. "So I read the synopsis [summary]. It had all the elements of a classic." Then Evens read the three chapters. She was drawn into the story and liked the humor in the writing. Evens asked Little if she could request the rest of the manuscript from Rowling. Evens was so enthusiastic that Little agreed.

Rowling was prepared for rejection when a letter arrived from the Christopher Little Literary Agency. One publisher and an agent had already refused the book. Rowling knew that the odds of getting a book published were not in her favor. Inside the envelope from the agency, she found the reply that would change her life. It requested the rest of her manuscript. That meant that the agent might help Rowling sell her book to a publisher. Rowling was stunned. "It was the best letter of my life," she later said. "I read it eight times."

Rowling sent off the rest of the book right away. Evens eagerly tore it open and started to read. She made some notes. Then she handed the manuscript to Little. He took it home and read it that very evening.

LITERARY AGENCIES

A writer who wants to get published needs to find a publisher. Often writers will hire an agent to help them with this process. A literary agent presents the writer's unpublished work to various publishing companies. Agents are especially helpful to first-time authors who may not understand the process. Most agencies have strong relationships with a variety of publishers.

An agency may consist of a single agent or many. Small agencies may focus only on a certain type of writing, such as science fiction. Larger agencies usually handle a wide variety of books. Agents take a part of the final sale of the writer's work as payment for their services. A good agent works not only to sell the writer's book but to get the best deal.

He returned to the office in the morning filled with enthusiasm for Rowling's book. Rowling had found her literary agent.

A PUBLISHER AT LAST

The Christopher Little Literary Agency worked on finding a publisher for Rowling's book. Meanwhile, Rowling continued to work on her education. The program grew more and more demanding as the school year went on. Rowling was student teaching by early 1996. At first, she wasn't a very good teacher. But she soon improved. Rowling's professors praised her ability to relate to students. They also liked her carefully planned and imaginative lessons. Rowling had a promising future as a classroom teacher.

Meanwhile, Bryony Evens continued to show *Harry Potter and the Philosopher's Stone* to publishers. Twelve publishers rejected the book. But thirteen would be a lucky number. Evens sent the manuscript to Bloomsbury. This publisher had recently started a children's book division. The head of the children's division was Barry Cunningham. He was wild about Rowling's book. "It was just terribly exciting," he later said. "What struck me first was that the book came with a fully imagined world. There was a complete sense of Jo knowing the characters and what would happen to them."

Cunningham convinced the company's directors to publish the book. They agreed to offer Rowling £1,500 ($2,250) for the rights to publish her book. She would also receive royalties for the book. This meant that Rowling would earn a small amount of money for each copy of the book that was sold. When Rowling heard the news, she screamed and leaped into the air with joy.

IT'S A FACT!

Many publishers felt Rowling's first book was too long for the middle-grade fiction market. These are fiction titles aimed at kids from the ages of nine through twelve. A typical middle-grade book is about forty thousand words. Rowling's draft was ninety thousand words. Bloomsbury took the chance that Rowling's long book would appeal to kids.

IN THE BOOKSHOPS

Editors at Bloomsbury got Rowling's book ready for publication. Meanwhile, Rowling finished her studies and started teaching. She took a part-time job at nearby Leith Academy. She had done her student teaching at that school over the summer. Leith Academy had a child care center where Rowling could leave Jessica while she taught. In between preparing lessons, Rowling started writing her second book. It would be called *Harry Potter and the Chamber of Secrets.* Rowling was still shy about her success as a writer. She told only those closest to her that her book was going to be published.

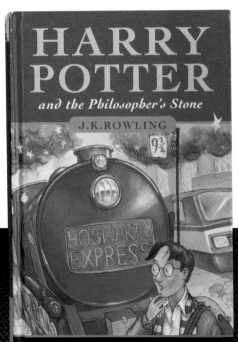

This is the cover of a rare first edition of *Harry Potter and the Philosopher's Stone.*

Rowling had always wanted to be a full-time writer. But this goal still seemed like just a dream. Rowling and her daughter couldn't live on her payment from Bloomsbury. And her part-time teaching salary was not enough to pay the bills.

By chance, she heard about a writer's grant offered by the Scottish Arts Council. To apply, she needed to be a resident of Scotland and a recently published author. *Harry Potter and the Philosopher's Stone* had not yet been published. But Rowling had a contract with Bloomsbury. The council agreed to consider her application. A judging panel was impressed with Rowling's strong proposal and writing samples. Rowling became one of forty finalists for the ten grants to be awarded. The council's panel granted Rowling their top award of £8,000 ($12,000). This money would support Rowling while she wrote *Harry Potter and the Chamber of Secrets.*

Rowling bought a computer when she received her check. She still wrote her drafts in longhand. But now she could use the computer to type and revise her next book.

Rowling's first manuscript was so well done that it required very little editing by Bloomsbury.

The biggest change Barry Cunningham wanted was in the author's name. He had been told that many boys didn't want to read books written by women. He thought both boys and girls would enjoy Rowling's book. So Joanne Rowling became J. K. Rowling. Rowling gave herself the middle name Kathleen after her favorite grandmother. When reporters later asked about the added initial, Rowling replied, "It was the publisher's idea. They could have called me Enid Snodgrass. I just wanted it [the book] published."

First published in Britain, Rowling's book (retitled *Harry Potter and the Sorcerer's Stone* in the United States) was soon in bookstores in the United States.

J. K. Rowling's *Harry Potter and the Philosopher's Stone* landed in Britain's bookstores on June 26, 1997. It had been seven long years since Harry Potter had popped into her head during a train ride. Rowling's lifelong dream had finally come true. She was a published author. "I walked around all day with a finished copy tucked under my arm," Rowling later recalled. "The first time I saw it in a bookshop I had this mad desire to sign it. It was an extraordinary moment."

CHAPTER 7

POTTERMANIA

(Above) Harry Potter fans come in all ages. These two British fans have dressed up as Harry Potter.

EVERY YEAR, PUBLISHERS from around the world gather at the Bologna Children's Book Fair in Italy. Many publishers search for foreign books to buy and publish in their own countries. An editorial director named Arthur Levine attended the show in 1997. He worked for the U.S. publisher Scholastic. Levine picked

up a story by an unknown British author named
J. K. Rowling. He read *Harry Potter and the
Philosopher's Stone* on the plane ride back to New
York City. Levine felt a connection to the story
right away. He decided to go after the rights to
publish the book in the United States.

The rights to publish a U.S. edition of
Rowling's book soon went up for sale in New York.
Levine found himself in a bidding war. The price
rose, and Levine asked himself "Do you love it this
much? Do you love it at $50,000? At $70,000?" In
the end, he won the bidding.

Levine agreed to pay $105,000 for the rights to
publish Rowling's first book. This was the largest
amount ever paid to a first-time children's author. It
was also the largest sum that Levine had ever paid
for a book. But he knew that Rowling's book was
worth the risk. "You have to follow your heart,"
Levine later said. "In Harry Potter, the wand
chooses the wizard; and when the wand chooses
you, you take it."

SUDDEN FAME

J. K. Rowling became famous overnight. People
began to know her as the single mother who had

risen from poverty to land a huge book deal. The press played up this Cinderella story. Reporters stretched the truth to make Rowling's story more dramatic. After all, Rowling had been on public assistance for only a brief time. She wasn't the newly divorced and penniless single mother that the press made her out to be. But Rowling's rags-to-riches story interested people. They read about her in newspaper stories and interviews. Sales of her book began to take off.

Rowling was not used to fame. But she was soon attending many events. Here, she attends the Glamour Magazine Women of the Year Awards in New York City in 1999.

The sudden fame was hard for Rowling. She wanted attention for her book, not for herself. Rowling experienced her first serious case of writer's block during this time. She was working hard on her second book, *Harry Potter and the Chamber of Secrets.* But she was having trouble deciding how to tell the story. "I was worried that it wouldn't live up to readers' expectations–I'd heard that your second novel is the hardest to write," Rowling said. Rowling delivered the second manuscript to her publisher two weeks after her first book was published. She had met her deadline, but she wasn't pleased with her work. So she convinced Bloomsbury to give the manuscript back to her. Rowling spent the next six weeks reworking and polishing the story. Then she set to work on the third book, *Harry Potter and the Prisoner of Azkaban.*

Harry Potter and the Philosopher's Stone moved up the best-seller list in Britain all summer. Both children and adults liked the story and the magical world Rowling had created. The book earned great reviews from critics. In November 1997, *Harry Potter and the Philosopher's Stone* received the Smarties Prize for outstanding children's literature. The book won several more awards. It was even the British Book Awards Children's Book of the Year. Rowling's fame grew, and sales of her novel soared. About seventy thousand copies of the book had sold in one year. Then *Harry Potter and the Chamber of Secrets* was released in Britain in July 1998. Right away, this book took the top spot on the best-seller list.

The second book has a theme of tolerance. Racist wizards believe there are different levels of wizards. They see pure-blooded wizards as the best. They call wizards who come from a mixed background of Muggles and wizards "mudbloods." This name is a big insult. Racist wizards call others in the magical world Squibs. This is a rude term for those from wizarding families who lack magical powers. Harry is faced

IT'S A FACT!

Only once has Rowling admitted to creating a character based completely on a real person. That character was Gilderoy Lockhart from *Harry Potter and the Chamber of Secrets.* He is the teacher of Defense Against the Dark Arts. Rowling refuses to say on whom Lockhart is based.

with prejudice in *Harry Potter and the Chamber of Secrets*. It forces him to think about tolerance and base his actions on his beliefs.

HARRY IN THE UNITED STATES

British readers were deep into the story of Harry Potter's second year at Hogwarts. But American audiences hadn't met the boy wizard yet. Scholastic published Rowling's first book in August 1998. It was titled *Harry Potter and the Sorcerer's Stone* for U.S. audiences. Readers in the United States liked the book just as much as readers in Britain did. Scholastic had ordered 190,000 copies of the book by the end of 1998. This was an amazing number of copies for a children's book. *Harry Potter and the Sorcerer's Stone* was one of the year's top sellers.

American readers soon found out that Rowling's second book was available in Britain. They started ordering it from overseas. Scholastic worried about losing sales. So the publisher started scrambling to publish *Harry Potter and the Chamber of Secrets*. The success of her book in the United States puzzled Rowling. She was surprised that U.S. audiences liked a book about a British boarding school. But the location didn't matter to readers.

They loved the story. Rowling's magical tale of friendship and good over evil had captured readers' imaginations.

Rowling put the payment from Scholastic in her bank account. And royalty checks began arriving. Rowling didn't need to worry so much about money anymore. She decided to make some changes in her life. She gave up her one-bedroom apartment and bought a larger place in Edinburgh. There, five-year-old Jessica would have her own bedroom for the first time. Rowling's new home was on a street called Hazelbank Terrace.

POTTER PROTESTS

The Harry Potter books are worldwide best sellers. But some people in the United States don't approve of them. The Harry Potter books often top the list of titles that people want banned from school libraries. Some Americans believe the stories are full of violence. Church groups have protested the books by burning them. Parents in many states have asked that Rowling's books be taken out of their children's schools.

Rowling finds the idea that her books approve of violence ridiculous. Many parents, teachers, and church leaders agree with her. Teachers and parents say they use the books to teach values such as loyalty, courage, honesty, and self-sacrifice. They say Rowling's stories encourage children to do what is right.

It was in a friendly neighborhood closer to Di. Rowling also left her teaching job and became a full-time writer. She had accomplished her lifelong goal.

Scholastic at last released *Harry Potter and the Chamber of Secrets* in the United States in July 1999. Bloomsbury released Rowling's third book that same month in Britain. *Harry Potter and the Prisoner of Azkaban* sold more than sixty thousand copies in the first three days. The third book hit the bookstores in the United States two months later. The Harry Potter books were worldwide best sellers by this time. Nearly thirty million copies were in print. And the books were available in twenty-seven languages. That summer, Rowling received her first £1 million ($1.5 million) royalty check.

Rowling's third book was all that fans on both sides of the Atlantic Ocean had hoped for. *Harry Potter and the Prisoner of Azkaban* has a darker mood, and the plot is more complicated. The book introduces Harry's godfather, Sirius Black. Sirius has escaped from Azkaban Prison. Readers also meet Remus Lupin. This new Defense Against the Dark Arts teacher was a friend of Harry's parents. The Dementors also make an appearance. They are the guards of Azkaban Prison. A kiss from a Dementor can erase happy memories and suck every bit of joy and hope out of a human soul. A teenage Harry is becoming more confident and is learning to fight evil. Harry also discovers that he must look hard for the truth. He shouldn't always believe what he sees and hears.

FANS AND A FILM DEAL

Fans were eager to meet the author who had created Harry Potter. So Rowling started to go to book signings. "The thing I enjoy best–apart from writing the books–is meeting the readers," she said.

Rowling often autographs her Harry Potter books at book signings.

"Answering their questions is pure pleasure." At these events, some fans bombard Rowling with all kinds of questions. Fans try to figure out small details in the books they've read or seek clues to future Harry Potter books. Other young fans are frozen with the excitement at meeting their favorite author.

Rowling went on a book tour in the United States in October 1999. Huge crowds showed up to meet her at events where she signed copies of her books. Long lines wound around the block. Some fans even camped out on the doorsteps of their local bookstores. They wanted to be first in line to meet Rowling. She was stunned. For the first time, Rowling realized just how much her books affected readers. She saw firsthand that people loved Harry Potter.

IT'S A FACT!

Rowling's young daughter Jessica was able to read the words "Harry" and "Potter." In bookstores, when she saw her mother's books, she would yell out the two words she knew. Rowling was embarrassed. She thought people might think she'd encouraged her daughter.

Hollywood also loved Harry Potter. Moviemakers approached Rowling shortly after *Harry Potter and the Sorcerer's Stone* was published. They wanted to buy the rights to make her book into a movie. But Rowling and agent Christopher Little decided the timing wasn't right. After all, Rowling was still writing the Harry Potter series. It would be confusing if a movie added characters or changed the story in any way. Rowling wanted a movie to stay true to the book. The setting had to be British. And all the actors had to be British too. At the end of 1999, Warner Bros. movie studio agreed. The studio struck a movie deal with Rowling for about $1 million. As part of the deal, Rowling would have a say in how the script was written. She would also have some control over the movie-related toys and games that could be sold.

BREAKING RECORDS

Rowling was very busy. But she tried to live a quiet and ordinary life. She took Jessica to school every morning. Then she hurried home to answer fan mail and phone calls. Rowling wasn't recognized by most people as she went about her daily life. She could spend her afternoons writing in a café. Then she returned home for tea and evenings with Jessica.

This daily routine changed midway through writing her fourth novel, *Harry Potter and the Goblet of Fire*. It was the hardest book she had written so far. Rowling ran into trouble with her well-planned plot. "The first three books, my plan never failed me. But I should have put that plot under a microscope. I wrote what I thought was half the book, and 'Ack!' Huge gaping hole in the middle of the plot." Rowling had to unwind her tightly woven plot and rewrite. Chapter nine frustrated her the most. She rewrote it thirteen times. Rowling worked for ten hours a day. But she still missed her deadline by two months.

Harry Potter and the Goblet of Fire was finally ready for release at midnight on July 8, 2000. It was available first in English-speaking countries, including Britain, the United States, and Canada. The book ends with an important plot twist. Rowling wanted to keep this ending secret until the book was published. So printers covered the books in brown paper before shipping them to booksellers. The books would only go to booksellers who promised not to open or sell a book before the release date. Excitement for *Harry Potter and the Goblet of Fire* soon built to a frenzy, called Pottermania. Hundreds of thousands of readers ordered the book online before it was actually available. Scholastic decided to order 3.8 million copies for the United States. This was the largest number of copies printed at one time for any book in history at that time.

In Britain, Rowling set off on a four-day tour to promote the book. She stepped out of a Ford Anglia at King's Cross Station in London to a crowd of five hundred cheering fans. From there, she traveled in an old-fashioned train. It was named the Hogwarts Express for the tour.

Rowling waves from the Hogwarts Express.

Lines of eager fans formed outside bookstores in the United States and Canada. They waited to buy the book at the stroke of midnight. Some bookstores held contests, parties, and other special events. One store in Vancouver, British Columbia, threw a party that drew about one thousand customers. Half of them had to be turned away because of overcrowding. A section of the Mall of America in Bloomington, Minnesota, became Potter Town. And a store in Portland, Oregon, offered 20 percent off for customers who showed up in their pajamas.

Readers started turning the pages of *Harry Potter and the Goblet of Fire* right away. In this book, Harry unexpectedly becomes a fourth contestant in the Triwizard Tournament. Three European wizarding schools are part of the tournament. The contestants use their magic skills to perform difficult tasks. Harry must draw on his courage and wits to survive the competition. Rowling's story grows darker and more emotional with this book. And there is a death for the first time.

8

LOOKING AHEAD

By the early 2000s, Rowling was world famous.

BY 2000, Rowling was overwhelmed by the enthusiasm of Harry Potter fans. She had seventy-six million copies of her books in print. She was fast becoming one of the wealthiest women in the world. Reporters were pounding on Rowling's door asking for interviews. And her picture was splashed on the covers of major news magazines. They included *Newsweek* in the United States and *Maclean's* in Canada. Rowling and her books were receiving many awards. Teachers and parents gave her credit for turning kids on to reading. Children who had never showed any interest in reading suddenly could not wait to pick up Rowling's books. All of her readers were eager for the next story about Harry Potter.

Rowling felt great pressure to begin her fifth book. But she was burned out. "The idea of going straight into another Harry Potter book filled me with dread and horror. And that was the first time I had ever felt like that," Rowling later said. She did not want a deadline. So her publishers agreed to let her work at her own pace.

Rowling took a long break from writing Harry Potter. She used most of that time to let the events of the past few years sink in. "I needed to stop and I needed to try to come to terms with what had happened to me," Rowling said. "For a long time people would say to me, 'What is it like to be famous?' and I would say, 'I am not famous.'" But she knew this wasn't true. She was famous, and she needed time to cope with that fact.

Rowling hadn't completely given up the world of Harry Potter, however. She was involved in the upcoming film version of *Harry Potter and the Philosopher's Stone*. This movie would be released as *Harry Potter and the Sorcerer's Stone* in the United States. Rowling worked with the screenwriter and sometimes visited the movie set to review scenes. Making sure the film was faithful to her book was important to her. Rowling also wrote two humorous books. They were *Quidditch through the Ages*, by Kennilworthy Whisp, and *Fantastic Beasts and Where to Find Them*, by Newt Scamander. In the Harry Potter books, these two titles are in the library at Hogwarts.

Rowling wrote and illustrated this tiny book. It was sold at a charity event.

COMIC RELIEF

Comic Relief began in 1985 to raise money for people around the world who suffer from abuse or poverty. Since then, more than two thousand professional comedians and entertainers have donated time to fund-raising events. The group has raised more than $590 million. The organization educates people about HIV and AIDS. It gives shots to children to help them guard against childhood diseases. It helps people who are victims of violence in their homes. About 80 percent of the profits for *Rowling's Fantastic Beasts and Where to Find Them* and *Quidditch through the Ages* went to Comic Relief.

Rowling donated the money from these books to the fund-raising group Comic Relief. The money supports aid organizations in Britain, in Africa, and around the world. These groups help people in poor countries.

LOVE AND CHARITY

Rowling was feeling lucky. She had Jessica. She had her writing. And she had financial security. She decided to buy a new home in Edinburgh. This mansion was covered in ivy. It had tall, stone walls for security and privacy. Rowling traveled to London often to meet with her agent and publisher. So she bought a home in that city too. Rowling was thankful for her good fortune. "I am fully aware, every single day, of how lucky I am," she said. "Lucky because I do not have to worry about my daughter's financial security any more; lucky because when what used to be Benefit Day [the day when benefit checks are given out] comes around there's still food in the fridge and the bills are paid."

In 2000, Rowling was very busy with work and her daughter. She had pushed the idea of finding love to the back of her mind. Then one evening, Rowling visited a friend. There she met a dark-haired doctor named Neil Murray. He had read ten pages of her first book during a late-night shift at the hospital. That was all he knew of Harry Potter. "And I thought that was fantastic," Rowling remembered. "He hadn't read the books. He didn't really have a very clear idea of who I was. It meant that we could get to know each other in quite a normal way."

Rowling spent much of her time with Jessica and Neil. She also started writing. But she worked on ideas other than Harry Potter. She also saved time for doing charity work. Her newfound fame and wealth gave her the chance to help causes she strongly believes in. Rowling became involved in the Multiple Sclerosis Society of Scotland and the National Council for One Parent Families. She donated

In 2000, Rowling became an ambassador for the National Council for One Parent Families in Britain.

money. And she also wrote articles and made speeches to support these organizations. A friend who had cancer inspired Rowling to raise money for cancer centers in Scotland. She donated items to be auctioned off and held book readings. Rowling became aware of how much influence she had.

HARRY HITS THE BIG SCREEN

In November 2001, Rowling and Murray attended the world premiere of *Harry Potter and the Philosopher's Stone* in London. The front of the theater had been turned into a copy of Hogwarts. Thousands of fans cheered the movie's cast and other celebrities as they walked the red carpet into the theater. Many people in the crowd dressed as wizards. The movie was all Rowling had hoped for. Everything was just as she had imagined, from the characters to Hogwarts to Quidditch.

All the actors were British. They made up what Rowling considered a "dream cast." She was very happy that Robbie Coltrane played Hagrid and Maggie Smith took the role of Professor McGonagall. She had especially wanted these actors cast in the movie. Alan Rickman played the dark and menacing Professor Snape. Richard Harris became the wise headmaster, Professor Dumbledore. Rupert Grint and Emma Watson were perfectly cast as Ron and Hermione. And Rowling saved especially high praise for Daniel Radcliffe. This young actor played Harry Potter. "What Daniel's got, I think, is the ability to listen and react very well on screen," Rowling commented. "Dan nailed it. And I am very pleased."

The movie earned mixed reviews. Many critics praised the special effects, set design, and acting. But nearly all agreed that the movie stayed too true to the book. It lacked creativity as a film. The movie was also long at two and a half hours. Still, fans of the book were thrilled. The magical story they loved was unfolding before their eyes. The movie was magic in other ways too. It set attendance records the first weekend. And it earned well over $300 million dollars by the following spring.

THE PHOENIX RISES

Rowling enjoyed living in Edinburgh. But she wanted to find some place where she could get away from the cameras and reporters. She wanted to find a peaceful setting where she could relax with her friends and family. A few weeks after the film premiere, Rowling purchased Killiechassie.

Rowling's retreat, Killiechassie, is in Scotland.

This mansion was built in 1865 on the River Tay in northern Scotland. Beautiful countryside surrounds the house. It was at Killiechassie that Joanne Rowling and Neil Murray married on December 26, 2001. Rowling had no time for a honeymoon, however. She was back to work on her fifth book. This one would be titled *Harry Potter and the Order of the Phoenix*. Rowling could no longer work in Edinburgh's cafés without people approaching her. Instead, she set up an office at home. Here, she would write all morning before taking a break for lunch. She wrote again until Jessica came home from school. Then it was family time with Jessica and Neil. In September 2002, Rowling announced that she was expecting her second child.

Rowling took time out from her writing in November. She attended the premiere of the next film, *Harry Potter and the Chamber of Secrets*. This movie was another smash hit with fans. Rowling returned to her writing right away. She was eager to finish the fifth book before the baby arrived. "I was getting bigger and bigger and bigger and then, just before Christmas, I realized I had finished the book and it was the most amazing thing," Rowling remembered. "It actually really took me by surprise. I was writing the last chapter, rewriting bits of it, as you do, and then I wrote myself to the end of a paragraph and thought, oh my God, I've finished the book! I couldn't believe I'd done it!" Three months later, Rowling's family celebrated the birth of David Gordon Rowling Murray.

Once again, the plot of the newest Harry Potter book was kept secret. Booksellers signed agreements not to sell the book until June 21, 2003. Pottermania reached a fever pitch. Scholastic prepared for the fans. The company ordered 8.5 million copies. This was a new record for the largest first printing of a book in history. Fans around the world snatched up *Harry Potter and the Order of the Phoenix* at the stroke of midnight on June 21. The book was Rowling's longest yet. The U.S. version weighed three pounds and was 870 pages long.

Harry Potter and the Order of the Phoenix was Rowling's darkest book yet. Harry is fifteen years old. He's very moody and often has angry outbursts. His fifth year at Hogwarts requires a lot of studying. At the same time, disagreement is growing in the wizarding world. Some believe the evil Voldemort is getting stronger. Others say that idea is nonsense. Among the believers is Professor Dumbledore. Among the naysayers is the head of the wizarding government and his supporters. They try to make those in the wizarding world doubt Dumbledore's words and actions. The Ministry of Magic appoints the nasty Dolores Umbridge as Defense Against the Dark Arts teacher and High Inquisitor of Hogwarts.

Harry Potter fans eagerly await the unpacking of *Harry Potter and the Order of the Phoenix* on June 21, 2003.

Umbridge sets out to make everyone's life miserable, especially Harry. Once again, Harry must face evil head on. And there is also a death. It pained Rowling to write the death scene.

LAUNCHING A WEBSITE

By early 2004, more than 250 million copies of Rowling's five Harry Potter books had been sold.

At the age of thirty-eight, Rowling joined the ranks of the wealthiest people in the world. Fame and fortune didn't affect Rowling much. Friends knew her as the same old Jo. She was witty and down to earth. And she had great passion for her family and for her writing. Rowling also felt strongly about connecting with her fans. She could no longer answer her enormous piles of fan mail. So she set up a

IT'S A FACT!

Kids had waited three years for *Harry Potter and the Order of the Phoenix*. They were ready to race through it. But some kids tried to read too much all at once. They came down with what one doctor called a "Hogwarts headache." Some parents had to force their children to take breaks from reading.

website at www.jkrowling.com. Here, Rowling
could share news and address false rumors. She
could also offer tidbits about her books.

IT'S A FACT!
In the first eight weeks, the website received 220 million visits from fans around the world.

Rowling announced the title of her next book on her website in the summer of 2004. It would be called *Harry Potter and the Half-Blood Prince.* Fans began talking about who might be the half-blood prince. But Rowling would say only that it is neither Harry Potter nor Voldemort. Rowling later announced on her website that she was expecting her third child. She assured fans that her pregnancy would not delay the sixth book.

The summer of 2004 also brought the film version of *Harry Potter and the Prisoner of Azkaban* to theaters. This movie earned great reviews from critics. Rowling said it was her favorite Harry Potter movie yet. Director Alfonso Cuaron presents a darker film filled with twisted humor. As with the previous Harry Potter movies, this one was a big winner. It broke attendance records the

Rowling and her husband, Neil Murray, went to the premiere of the movie *Harry Potter and the Prisoner of Azkaban* together in May 2004.

opening weekend. And the film earned about $250 million by the time the DVD came out in November 2004.

Over the next few months, Rowling posted big news on her website. On December 20, she told fans that she had sent her sixth manuscript to her publishers. The next day, Rowling's publishers announced that the sixth book, *Harry Potter and the Half-Blood Prince,* would be published on July 16, 2005. On that date, it

IT'S A FACT!

Rowling's British publisher used forest-friendly paper to print *Harry Potter and the Half-Blood Prince*. Her U.S. publisher again topped the mark in its first print run. Scholastic printed 10.8 million copies. They ran a second printing before the first printing even went on sale.

would be available in bookstores in the United States, Canada, Britain, and Australia.

Rowling said that the first chapter had been brewing in her mind for thirteen years. Book six picks up where *Harry Potter and the Order of the Phoenix* left off. There is a war heating up between the forces of good and evil in the wizarding world.

A month after delivering her latest Harry Potter book, Rowling gave birth to a baby girl. Mackenzie Jean Rowling Murray arrived on January 23, 2005. "She is ridiculously beautiful, though I suppose I might be biased," Rowling said on her website.

THE END OF THE STORY

Harry Potter has been with Rowling since he first entered her head in 1990. She will reach the end of her journey with the boy wizard when she finishes the seventh book. "It has been such a massive part of my life now. I can see myself being really scared to let go of it. I will probably reach the end of seven and think, 'I'll just tweak it a bit more,'" Rowling said. "The fact that I will have finished will be extraordinary."

What is even more extraordinary is how Harry Potter has changed Rowling's life and the lives of her readers. She was a bookish girl with a love of stories. Then she became a teacher and a single mother. These days, Rowling is one of the most famous and beloved authors in the world. She has inspired a generation of children to read and to use their imaginations. And she has shown how hard work, determination, and a little luck can lead to magical results.

Over the years, Rowling has changed only small details from the original plan for her story. It is still all about Harry. "He really is the whole story," she explained. Rowling has known the end of her tale for years. But she has not and will not tell a soul. In fact, she has already written the final chapter and tucked it away in a safety deposit box. She won't say whether the ending

Rowling smiles at the book launch of the sixth Harry Potter book on July 16, 2005.

will be happy for Harry and his friends. But she has said that the last word is *scar*.

As for herself, Rowling is happier than she has ever been. A loving family surrounds her, and she is able to focus on her life's goal. She will leave Harry Potter behind someday. But Rowling knows one thing for sure. "I'll be writing until I can't write anymore."

activist: a person who is actively involved in bringing about change

Amnesty International: an international nongovernmental organization that works to promote human rights all over the world. In particular, Amnesty International works to end the death penalty, torture, and other cruel treatment of prisoners.

boarding school: a private school where students live during the school year. A boarding school house–such as Gryffindor House–is a place where the students have their rooms for sleeping and studying.

Church of England: the organization that oversees the main form of Christianity that is followed in England

diagnosis: a doctor's identification of a disease by its signs (symptoms) and by laboratory tests

dissertation: a lengthy paper on a specialized subject. The paper is required before a person can get a degree.

Fascist: a national system in which the government has all the power. It is usually headed by an all-powerful dictator. The nation is viewed as more important than the individuals that make up the nation.

Hell's Angels: the oldest and biggest original motorcycle club in the world. The club was founded in 1948 in San Bernardino, California.

human rights: rights to which people are entitled simply because they are human beings, regardless of their nationality, race, ethnicity, gender, or religion

manuscript: a written or typewritten document that has not yet been published

Quidditch: a magical ball game played in the air on broomsticks. In Rowling's Harry Potter books, each house has a Quidditch team.

rights: in publishing, the identification of who owns a piece of writing or illustration

Royal Navy: the navy of the United Kingdom. It operates a number of aircraft carriers, destroyers, frigates, fifteen nuclear submarines, and various other ships.

royalties: a percentage of the profits from the sale of each copy of a book that goes to the author or illustrator

screenwriter: the person who writes the script for a movie. The writer either adapts an existing work for production as a movie or creates a new screenplay.

social justice: a belief that governments are created for the benefit of the members of the state or nation and that those governments that fail to see to the welfare of their citizens are failing to fulfill their role

tolerance: sympathy or indulgence for beliefs or practices differing from or conflicting with one's own

unsolicited: something that is not asked for

welfare: an agency or program that helps those in need by providing money for food, clothing, and shelter

SOURCE NOTES

10–11 J. K. Rowling, "J. K. Rowling at the Edinburgh Book Festival." *J. K. Rowling Official Site*, August 15, 2004, http://www.jkrowling .com/textonly/news_view.cfm?id =80 (July 22, 2005).

12–13 Lindsey Fraser, *Conversations with J. K. Rowling* (New York: Scholastic, 2000), 15.

13 J. K. Rowling, "The Not Especially Fascinating Life So Far of J. K. Rowling," *Cliphoto.com*, 2001, http://www.cliphoto.com/ potter/rowling.htm (July 22, 2005).

14 Fraser, 13.

15 Rowling, "The Not Especially Fascinating Life So Far of J. K. Rowling."

16 Fraser, 23.

17 Ibid., 22.

18 Rowling, "The Not Especially Fascinating Life So Far of J. K. Rowling."

18–19 Fraser, 18.

21 Ibid., 28.

21 J. K. Rowling, "First Person," *Scotsman.com*, April 22, 2001, http://www.entertainment.scots man.com/headlines_specific.cfmi ?d=2109 (July 25, 2005).

22 J. K. Rowling, "Biography" *J. K. Rowling Official Site*, n.d., http://www.jkrowling.com/texton ly/biography.cfm (July 22, 2005).

24 Ibid.

29 Rowling, "The Not Especially Fascinating Life So Far of J. K. Rowling."

30 J. K. Rowling, live Web chat, *World Book Day Festival*, March 4,

2004, http://www.worldbookday festival.com/2004/jkrowling.html (July 25, 2005).

30 Rowling, "The Not Especially Fascinating Life So Far of J. K. Rowling."

31 "Discovering the Real World of Harry Potter," *American Public Television*, 2002.

31 Rowling, "Biography" *J. K. Rowling Official Site*

32 Fraser, 38.

33 J. K. Rowling "Chat Transcript," *Barnesandnoble.com*, March 19, 1999, http://search.barnesand noble.com/booksearch/isbn inquiry.asp?userid=a11E69SAm X&ean=9780590353403&pwb= 1&displayonly=ITV#ITV (July 25, 2005).

34–35 J. K. Rowling, "FAQ," *J. K. Rowling Official Site*, n.d., http://www.jkrowling.fr/textonly/ faq_view.cfm?id=12 (July 25, 2005).

36 J. K. Rowling, "Extra Stuff," *J. K. Rowling Official Site*, n.d., http://www.jkrowling.com/texton ly/extrastuff_view.cfm?id=7 (July 25, 2005).

38 J. K. Rowling, "A Good Scare: The Wizard of Harry Potter Explains What Kids Need to Know of the Dark Side," *Time.com*, Oct. 30, 2000, http:// www.time.com/time/pacific/mag azine/20001030/potter.html (July 25, 2005).

40 Margaret Weir, "Of Magic and Single Motherhood," *Salon.com*, March 31, 1999, http://www .salon.com/mwt/feature/1999/

03/cov_31featureb.html (July 22, 2005).

45 Rowling, "First Person."

45 J. K. Rowling, "I Miss My Mother So Much," *National Multiple Sclerosis Society*, 2001, http://www.nationalmssociety.org /%5CIMSSu02-MyMother.asp (July 25, 2005).

45 Rowling, "Biography."

47–48 Ibid.

49 Weir.

50 Angela Levin, "The Penniless Mother behind Harry Potter," *Daily Mail* (London), July 9, 1999, 13.

52 Simon Hattenstone, "Harry, Jessie and Me," *Guardian*, July 8, 2000, http://www.guardian.co.uk /weekend/story/0,,340821,00 .html (July 22, 2005).

54 Sean Smith, *J. K. Rowling: The Genius behind Harry Potter* (London: Arrow Books, 2002), 139.

55 Hattenstone.

56 Ibid.

57 Rowling, "Biography."

58–59 Levin.

60–61 Tom Peterkin, "How 4,000 Loan Gave Rise to Harry Potter," *Telegraph.co.uk*, March 22, 2004, http://www.telegraph.co.uk/ news/main.jhtml?xml=/news/ 2004/03/22/npott22.xml (July 25, 2005).

64–65 "Bryony Evens: Saved Harry Potter from the Reject Pile," *People*, April 12, 2004.

66 Nigel Reynolds, "£100,000 Success Story for Penniless Mother," *Telegraph.co.uk*, July 7, 1997, http://www.telegraph.co .uk/htmlContent.jhtml?html=/arc hive/1997/07/07/nbuk07.html (July 25, 2005).

67 Smith, 159.

70 Richard Savill, "Harry Potter and the Mystery of J. K.'s Lost Initial," *Telegraph.co.uk*, July 19, 2000 http://www.telegraph.co .uk/news/main.jhtml?xml=/new /2000/07/19/npot19.xml (July 25, 2005).

71 Fraser, 46.

73 Arthur A. Levine, "Why I Paid So Much," *The New York Times*, October 13, 1999, C16.

73 Ibid.

75 Fraser, 48.

80–81 Ibid., 53.

83 Jeff Jensen, "'Fire' Storm," *Entertainment Weekly*, September 7, 2000, http://www.ew.com/ew/ report/0,6115,85523_5|6999||0_0 _,00.html (July 25, 2005).

87 Ann Treneman, "Hogwarts and All: The J. K. Rowling Interview," *Sunday Herald*, June 22, 2003, http://www.sunday herald.com/34715 (July 25, 2005).

87 Ibid.

89–90 J. K. Rowling, "A Kind of Magic," *Telegraph.co.uk*, June 9, 2002, http://www.telegraph.co .uk/core/Content/displayPrint able.jhtml?xml=/health/2002 /06/10/fmrowl09.xml&site=13 (July 25, 2005).

90 Treneman.

92 Andrew Alderson, "They Really Do Look as I'd Imagined They Would in My Head."

Telegraph.co.uk, November 4,
2001, http://www.telegraph.co
.uk/news/main.jhtml?xml=/
news/2001/11/04/npot04.xml
(July 25, 2005).

92 Ibid.

94–95 Treneman.

97 "Harry Potter Causing Hogwarts
Headaches?" *CNN.com*, October
29, 2003, http://www.cnn.com/
2003/HEALTH/10/29/offbeat
.hogwarts.headaches.ap/ (July 25,
2005).

100 J. K. Rowling, "JKR Gives Birth
to Baby Girl," *J. K. Rowling
Official Site*, January 25, 2005,
http://www.jkrowling.com/
textonly/news_view.cfm?id=83
(July 25, 2005).

101 Treneman.

101 Rowling, "J. K. Rowling at the
Edinburgh Book Festival."

102 "J. K. Rowling Discusses the
Surprising Success of 'Harry
Potter,'" *CNN.com Transcripts*,
October 20, 2000, http://
transcripts.cnn.com/
TRANSCRIPTS/0010/20/
lkl.00.html (July 25, 2005).

Selected Bibliography

Books

Beahm, George. *Muggles and Magic: J. K. Rowling and the Harry Potter Phenomenon.* Charlottesville, VA: Hampton Roads Publishing Co., 2004.

Fraser, Lindsey. *Conversations with J. K. Rowling.* New York: Scholastic, 2000.

Schafer, Elizabeth D. *Exploring Harry Potter.* Osprey, FL: Beacham Publishing, 2000.

Smith, Sean. J. K. Rowling: *The Genius behind Harry Potter.* London: Arrow Books, 2002.

Internet Sites:

Rowling, J. K. *J. K. Rowling Official Site-Harry Potter and More.* N.d.http://www.jkrowling.com (May 2005).

Rowling, J. K. *The Not Especially Fascinating Life So Far of J. K. Rowling.* http://www.cliphoto.com/potter/rowling.htm

Rowling, J. K. Transcript of live interview on Scholastic.com, October 16, 2000. http://www.scholastic.com/harrypotter/author/transcript2.htm

Rowling, J. K. Live Web chat, *World Book Day Festival,* March 4, 2004. http://www.worldbookdayfestival.com2004/jkrowling_chat.html (May 2005).

Magazines and News Articles:

Feldman, Roxanne. "The Truth about Harry." *School Library Journal,* September 1999, 136.

Rowling, J. K., "First Person." *Scotsman.com.* April 22, 2001.

Treneman, Ann. "J. K. Rowling: The Interview." *Times* (London), June 30, 2000.

Weir, Margaret. "Of Magic and Single Motherhood." *Salon.com.* March 31, 1999 (May 2005).

FURTHER READING AND WEBSITES

Adler, Bill, ed. *Kid's Letters to Harry Potter from around the World.* New York: Carroll & Graf Publishers, Inc., 2001.

Alton, Steve. *The Firehills.* Minneapolis: Carolrhoda Books, Inc., 2005.

Alton, Steve. *The Malifex.* Minneapolis: Carolrhoda Books, Inc., 2003.

J. K. Rowling Official Site
http://www.jkrowling.com
The official website of the Harry Potter series and author J. K. Rowling. Includes FAQ, news, links to fan sites, biography, and much more. Officiated by J. K. Rowling herself.

Kronzek, Allan Zola. *The Sorcerer's Companion: A Guide to the Magical World of Harry Potter.* New York: Broadway Books, 2001.

Rowling, J. K. *Harry Potter and the Chamber of Secrets.* New York: Scholastic, 1999.

Rowling, J. K. *Harry Potter and the Goblet of Fire.* New York: Scholastic, 2000.

Rowling, J. K. *Harry Potter and the Half-Blood Prince.* New York: Scholastic, 2005.

Rowling, J. K. *Harry Potter and the Order of the Phoenix.* New York: Scholastic, 2003.

Rowling, J. K. *Harry Potter and the Prisoner of Azkaban.* New York: Scholastic, 1999.

Rowling, J. K. *Harry Potter and the Sorcerer's Stone.* New York: Scholastic, 1998.

Scamander, Newt [J. K. Rowling]. *Fantastic Beasts and Where to Find Them.* New York: Scholastic and Obscurus Books, 2001.

Whisp, Kennilworthy [J. K. Rowling]. *Quidditch through the Ages.* New York: Scholastic and Whizzhard Books, 2001.

INDEX

Scotland, 90
multiple sclerosis, 22, 44, 90
Murray, David Gordon Rowling
  (son), 95
Murray, Mackenzie Jean
  Rowling (daughter), 100
Murray, Neil, 90, 94

names, 30, 34–35
National Council for One Parent
  Families, 90

Porto, Portugal, 46–51, 58
Potter, Ian and Vicki, 9
pottermania. *See* fans
Prewett, Jill, 46–47, 49, 51

Quidditch Through the Ages, 88, 89
Quidditch, 36

Rodrigues, Marília, 49
Rowling, Anne Volant (mother),
  6–12, 21–22, 44–45; death of,
  45, 47–48
Rowling, Dianne "Di" (sister), 8,
  13, 14, 16, 17, 50, 54, 56–57, 79
Rowling, Ernie (grandfather), 13
Rowling, Jessica (daughter), 50,
  51, 52, 53, 55, 57, 58, 59, 68,
  81, 82–83, 89, 90, 94
Rowling, J. K. (Joanne, "Jo"):
  advice to writers, 30;
  appearance of, 16; artwork of,
  17, 88; birth and childhood of,
  8–24; book signings and tours,
  4–5, 80–81, 84; and charity, 89,
  90–91; earnings from Harry
  Potter series, 67, 78, 79, 82, 97;
  education of, 10, 13, 14–15,
  18–, 23, 24–27, 59–60, 66;
  employment of, 28–30 46, 66,
  67–68, 79; fame and success, 6,
  73–75, 86–87, 93, 97, 101; and
  fans, 86, 97–98; favorite books

of, 17, 19, 27, 49; friendships of,
  9, 14–15, 18, 23–24, 25–26,
  46–47, 60–61; homes of, 78, 93.
  See also Church Cottage;
  inspiration of characters, 14,
  23, 36, 76; and marriage, first,
  50–51, 58–59; and marriage,
  second, 94; and mothers death,
  47–49; and music, 23, 26;
  name change, 70; and name
  collecting, 34–35; personality
  of, 16, 18, 87; in Portugal,
  46–51; and poverty, 54–56;
  similarities to characters, 35,
  37–38; and writer's block, 75;
  and writing first Harry Potter,
  30–33, 39, 47–49, 50, 57, 59,
  60, 63
Rowling, Kathleen
  (grandmother), 13
Rowling, Pete (father), 6–9,
  11–12, 44–45, 52

Scholastic, 72, 77, 79, 84, 95, 100
Scottish Arts Council, 69
Shepherd, Lucy, 18–19
Snape, Severus, 42–43, 92

Volant, Frieda (grandmother), 14
Volant, Stanley (grandfather), 14
Voldemort, 35, 38, 98

Warner Bros., 82. *See also* Harry
  Potter movies
Weasley, Ron, 32, 36, 42
website, 97–98
welfare system, 54, 55

111

PHOTO ACKNOWLEDGMENTS

The images in this book are used with permission of: © AFP/Getty Images, p. 6; © Liam Dale Television, pp. 7, 11, 12, 25; © Hulton-Deutsch Collection/CORBIS, p. 20; Library of Congress, (LC-USZ62-74760), p. 27; © Gary Hansen/Independent Picture Service, p. 28; © Bryan Pickering; Eye Ubiquitous/CORBIS, p. 36; © Warner Bros./ZUMA Press, pp. 34, 37; © Avantis/ZUMA Press, p. 43; © age fotostock.com/SuperStock, pp. 46, 53; © Murdo Macleod/CORBIS SYGMA, p. 48; The University of Edinburgh, p. 59; © Barclay Graham/CORBIS SYGMA, p. 62; © Getty Images, pp. 68, 70; © AP/Wide World Photos, p. 72; © Mitchell Gerber/CORBIS, p. 74; © Reuters/CORBIS, pp. 80, 86, 96; © Joe Alvarez/Alpha/Globe Photos, Inc., p. 84; © Toby Melville/Reuters/CORBIS, p. 88; © UPPA/ZUMA Press, p. 91; © Randolph Caughie/Alpha/Globe Photos, Inc., p. 93; © MWPress/ZUMA Press, p. 99; © Simon Hollington/UPPA/ZUMA Press, p. 102.

Cover image: © Mike Marsland/WireImage.com.